EXPLORE THE
W**RLD**

PHYSICAL SCIENCE

Fairy-Tale
Science

CHARLENE BRUSSO

TABLE OF CONTENTS

PIONEER VALLEY EDUCATIONAL PRESS, INC

ONCE UPON A TIME

Could anyone really sleep for 100 years? Dance in glass slippers? Get golden eggs from a goose? Could science ever make fairy-tale magic come true?

Actually, many things we do every day would seem magical to the people who made up Cinderella and Sleeping Beauty. Hundreds of years ago, the idea of a screen that shows you stories, an object that lets you talk to people around the world, or a machine that flies through the air would have sounded like pure fantasy. Yet televisions, cell phones, and airplanes are all normal now. Science has made those dreams real.

So what else could science do?

SLEEPING BEAUTY

Have you ever wished you could cast spells—just say something and have it come true? Maybe it's just as well you can't. The next time you borrow your sister's skates without asking, she could put you to sleep for 100 years like Sleeping Beauty!

Could anyone really sleep for 100 years? Probably not. But there are animals that take some extremely long naps. Bears, groundhogs, mice, and snakes **hibernate** through the winter, so they sleep for months at a time. A hibernating animal slows down its breathing and heart rate. It also lowers its body temperature and doesn't eat or drink. Then, when the weather warms, it wakes up.

If scientists can figure out what happens in an animal's body during hibernation, maybe one day we could hibernate too. This would be great for astronauts, allowing them to sleep through long space voyages.

6

But animals keep growing older, even when they hibernate. So, if a real Sleeping Beauty ever did manage to hibernate for 100 years, she might wake up as Sleeping Grandma!

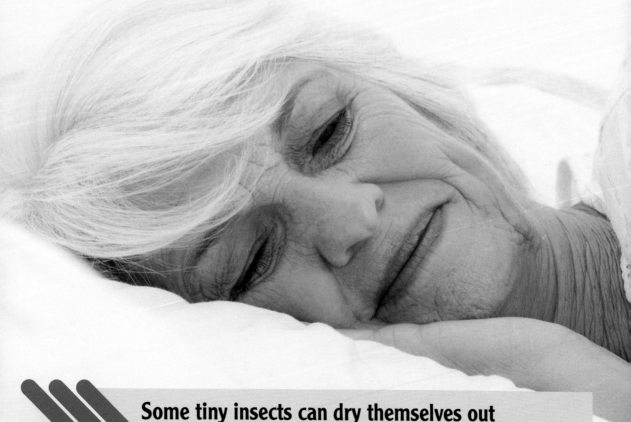

>>> **Some tiny insects can dry themselves out and remain dormant for many years at a time.**

GLASS SLIPPERS

They may look sparkly, but would you really want shoes made of glass? They would be hard, slippery, and likely to shatter when you stepped in them.

But glassmakers have discovered ways to make glass extra tough by heating and then quickly cooling it. This glass is strong and scratchproof. And when it does break, it shatters into small chunks instead of knife-sharp **shards**.

You don't have to go to a ball to see this magical glass. It's all around you—in car windows, cell phones, and computers. Who knows? Maybe someday, even shoes.

GROWING GEMS

In the story "Toads and Diamonds," a fairy rewards a kind girl with a spell that makes gems fall from her mouth when she speaks. We probably won't ever be able to pull gems from thin air, but we can create them in a laboratory.

To grow gems, scientists melt minerals in a hot furnace.
As the liquid cools, it slowly forms crystals.

TALKING TO ANIMALS

Where would all those lost princesses be without their kind animal helpers? And it's so convenient that they can talk!

In the real world, communicating with animals isn't quite so easy—yet. But scientists are making a lot of progress, and it will not be long before we crack the code. Soon you may be able to tell what it means when a bird tweets, a dog wags its tail, and a dolphin whistles. The next step after that will be to learn how to talk back.

Of course, even when we learn to talk to animals, that doesn't mean animals think like people. They have very different minds. They're more likely saying, "This is my tree, back off!" than giving directions to the nearest castle.

Animals communicate not only with sounds but with gestures and smells as well.

LET DOWN YOUR HAIR

Poor Rapunzel, **imprisoned** in a tower, must lower her long braid of hair to let visitors in. But could a person's hair really hold a prince?

Yes! And you don't even need any magic. Plain old hair is quite strong. A single strand can hold 3 ounces. That is the weight of four mice. And an average head has about 120,000 hairs. Tie all those hairs together in a braid and you'll have a rope that could hold a couple of elephants. A prince? No problem.

MORE TO EXPLORE

In real life, human hair only grows a few feet long at most.

THE LONGEST HAIR EVER

measured was about 18 feet. That's pretty long for hair—but pretty short for a tower.

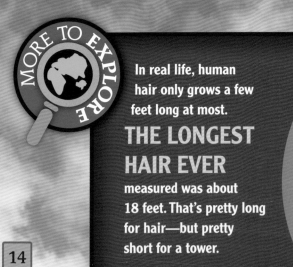

UP, UP, AND AWAY

So how about wings or a nice broomstick? Will people ever be able to fly?

Inventors have been tinkering with one-person flying machines for hundreds of years, but none are quite ready for everyday use.

MORE TO EXPLORE

The Martin Jetpack, made by a company in New Zealand, looks like a **BACKPACK** with two big fans. It can fly up to 46 miles per hour.

One engineer has made a carpet fly. His carpet is actually two small sheets of plastic stuck together. Electricity from a small battery makes the sheets **vibrate** at different rates, creating a rippling motion. That motion causes the carpet to float through the air like a stingray over the ocean floor.

INVISIBILITY CLOAK

When sneaking into an ogre's castle, it's always handy to have an **invisibility** cloak that lets you walk unseen. You'll be glad to know that scientists are hard at work on a real one. So far, it's more like a box than a cloak, and they've only managed to hide very small objects. But soon, hide-and-seek may never be the same.

Another way to become invisible is to camouflage yourself so that you look exactly like the background. Some animals are quite good at this. Though it doesn't exist yet, it's possible that someday a special fabric may be able to sense what is behind you and change its colors to match.

GLOSSARY

dormant
not active

hibernate
to spend the winter sleeping or resting

imprisoned
trapped

invisibility
the state of not being visible

shards
sharp pieces of something, such as glass or pottery

vibrate
to move very quickly back and forth from side to side

INDEX

19

20

SPINNING STRAW INTO GOLD

COULD YOU EVER SPIN GOLD OUT OF STRAW LIKE RUMPLESTILTSKIN?

It isn't really possible to *make* gold.

But some researchers have come up with a way to draw gold from wheat, alfalfa, and oats. These plants absorb tiny bits of metal from the soil. By extracting the metal from the plants, the researchers may have found a new way to mine for gold!